Finding the Way

How to become a Christian

PAUL MOULD

Cover image: https://steemit.com/life/@mawit07/two-roads-in-life-the-right-and-wrong-paths (also p.14)

DEDICATION

To my Lord and Savior Jesus Christ: "The Son of God, who loved me and gave Himself for me" Galatians 2:20 (NIV)

ACKNOWLEDGEMENTS

Special thanks go to "The Navigators" organization, who first introduced me to the 'Bridge Diagram' over 40 years ago. I am also very grateful to all who have since inspired me in the task of telling people the good news of the Gospel of Jesus Christ.

CONTENTS

INTRODUCTION

Where are you going in life? There seem to be many possible roads to take – but where do they all lead? Is there a way to find God?

The Bible tells us that there is a right way and a wrong way in life. It's easy to make the wrong choice: "There is a path before each person that seems right, but it ends in death." (Proverbs 14:12 NLT).

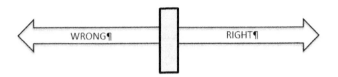

The right way that leads to life and the wrong way leads to death. How can we find the way to life?

1. THE WRONG WAY

The wrong way is doing our own thing, living life our own way. This is life without giving God his rightful place. Sin is all the bad stuff that we do, say or think. Going the wrong way only leads to sadness and an alienation from God, who loves us. The truth is that sin separates us from God; it is like there is a great chasm between us and God, with no way to cross over.

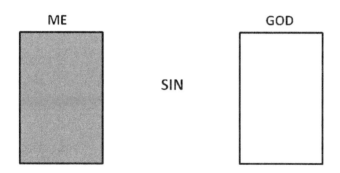

There is nothing I can do to get across the sin 'chasm'; there is no way to bridge the huge gap between ourselves and God. Doing good, trying my best, or being religious can't deal with the problem; these things can never cancel out sin. Sin is like a massive roadblock on the way to a relationship with God.

2. THE RIGHT WAY

The Bible says "For God so loved the world that he gave his one and only Son, that whoever believes in him shall not perish but have eternal life." (John 3:16, NIV).

We need a way to bridge the chasm created by our sin, something that can span the gap between us and God. Because He loves us so much, God provided a way for us to 'cross-over' - which is the Cross where Jesus died for us. Our sin had to be punished, but on the Cross Jesus took that punishment for us and so made a way for us to come to know and experience a relationship with God the Father. All our sin has been put on Jesus.

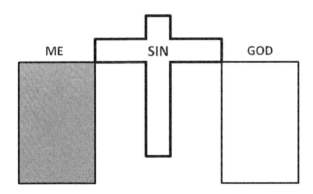

Jesus said "I am the Way...no one can come to the Father except through me."(John 14:6 NLT). We can only come to God through Jesus and through the Cross. The sin problem has been dealt with, so now we can cross over from death to life (John 5:24).

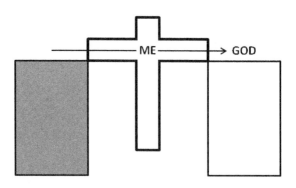

We choose the right way when we put our trust in what Jesus has done for us. We can receive forgiveness and eternal life as a free gift. This truth is summed up in an old hymn:

"There's a way back to God from the dark paths of sin;
There's a door that is open and you may go in:
At Calvary's cross is where you begin,
When you come as a sinner to Jesus"[1]

God offers the way to a new life and a new hope for the future. Because Jesus rose from the dead and defeated death, he offers us an eternal life, living with Him for ever. There is joy and peace in going the right way. All our sin is forgiven, and guilt and shame are gone.

3. CHOOSING THE WAY

"God says, 'At just the right time, I heard you. On the day of salvation, I helped you.' Indeed, the "right time" is now. Today is the day of salvation." (2 Corinthians 6:2, NIV).

Is now the time for you to choose God's way? Why not grab the opportunity today? None of us is promised tomorrow; so consider carefully which way to choose. Don't put off the decision for another day.

This is what God requires us to do:

1. Turn away from everything wrong and turn to Him.
2. Believe that Jesus died on the cross so that your sin could be forgiven.
3. Receive God's forgiveness.
4. Give control of your life over to Jesus so that He is the Boss (Lord).

If you would like to become a Christian please pray the following prayer:

"Dear Father God,
Thank you for sending Jesus to die for my sin,
Today I turn away from everything that is wrong,
And now I turn to you.
Please forgive me of all my sin
And give me a new life.
Thank you for loving me.
Today I give my life to you, I choose your way.
In Jesus' name, Amen."

If you sincerely meant that prayer you can be sure that you have started a new life. The Bible says: "Anyone who belongs to Christ has become a new person. The old life is gone; a new life has begun!" 2 Corinthians 5:17 (NLT).

You have now entered into a new relationship with God.

4. WHAT'S NEXT?

First, *speak up* about your faith in Jesus by talking to someone about what you have done, perhaps the person who gave you this booklet, or someone you know who is a Christian. Find a lively church, especially one that hosts an Alpha Course (a series of interactive sessions that freely explore the basics of the Christian faith; https://alpha.org.uk). Then *grow* your faith by going on an Alpha Course (or something similar); you may also find my book "Secure Foundations: An Introductory Course for New Christians"[2] helpful. Finally, *share* your faith – it's good news, too good to keep for yourself!

REFERENCES

1. Swinstead, E. H. "There's a way back to God" https://hymnary.org/media/fetch/190709. The word "Calvary" is derived from the Latin name for the place where Jesus died.

2. Mould, P. "Secure Foundations: An Introductory Course for New Christians" Amazon Publishing 2021.

ABOUT THE AUTHOR

Paul hails from Leicestershire, England, but has spent almost all his adult life in the Manchester area. He formerly worked in Biochemistry, Cell Biology and Biophysics at the University of Manchester, UK. Following his recent retirement he has acted as a Trustee of a local Foodbank and taken up his passion for Christian writing. This book is the first in a series of books he has written on Christian Foundations. Paul and his wife have three children and six lively grandchildren.

Correspondence e-mail: apaulmould@hotmail.co.uk

PREVIOUS BOOKS BY THE AUTHOR

Mould, Paul "Secure Foundations: An Introductory Course for New Christians", Kindle Edition 2021.

Mould, Paul "Secure Foundations: An Introductory Course for New Christians", Paperback Edition 2021. Amazon Publishing ISBN: 9798787984224

Mould, Paul "The Hope of Glory: The Wonderful Future Promised to Christians" Kindle Edition 2021.

Mould, Paul "The Hope of Glory: The Wonderful Future Promised to Christians" Paperback Edition 2022. Amazon Publishing ISBN: 9798442123074.

Mould, Paul. "Honouring the Holy Spirit". Kindle Edition 2021.

Mould, Paul. "Honouring the Holy Spirit". Paperback Edition 2021. Amazon Publishing ISBN: 9798479238550.

Mould, Paul "Revival in Manchester 1859-74. The thrilling, untold story" Kindle Edition 2021.

Mould, Paul "Revival in Manchester 1859-74. The thrilling, untold story" Paperback Edition 2021. Amazon Publishing ISBN: 9798768944087.

Mould, Paul "Dangerous Doctrines of Hypergrace. A Brief Guide and Rebuttal". Paperback Edition 2022. Amazon Publishing ISBN: 9798831858112.

Mould, Paul "Dangerous Doctrines of Hypergrace. A Brief Guide and Rebuttal". Kindle Edition 2022.

NOTES

Printed in Great Britain
by Amazon

86461271R00020